Contents

Landforms

The land is made of different shapes.
These shapes are called landforms.

volcano

A volcano is a landform.
Volanoes are found all over the world.

What is a volcano?

A volcano is a mountain with a hole on the top.

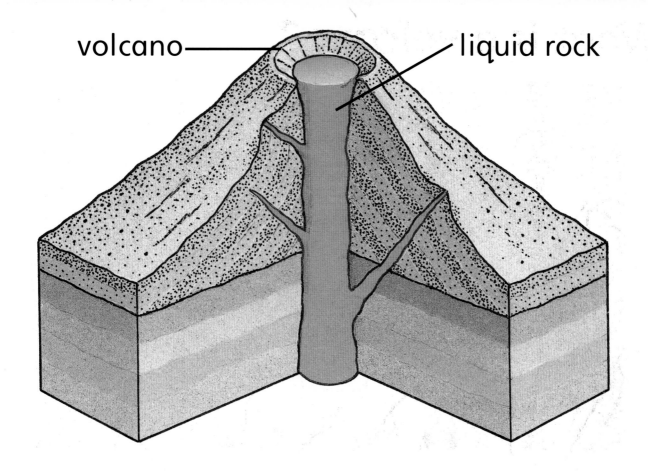

volcano — liquid rock

The hole goes down deep into the Earth. Deep in the Earth is a layer of rock which is so hot it is a liquid.

The hot liquid can rush up the hole and erupt out of the top of the volcano.

The liquid rock is called lava.

When the lava has erupted out of the volcano it cools down and becomes hard.

Every time the volcano erupts,
a new layer of lava is left on
the mountain.

Features of a volcano

crater

The hole at the top of a volcano
is called a crater.

cone

Some volcanoes have a cone-shaped top.

Where are volcanoes found?

Some volcanoes are in hot countries.

Some volcanoes are in cold countries.

Some islands are the cones of underwater volcanoes.

Some countries have lots of volcanoes close together.

What lives near a volcano?

After an eruption, the land around a volcano is good for growing things.

Many plants grow in the soil.

Some people live near volcanoes but they have to watch out. The volcano might erupt!

Studying volcanoes

Some people study volcanoes. They check if they are about to erupt.

Volcanoes remind us that deep in the Earth there is a layer of liquid rock.

Volcano facts

Mauna Loa is a volcano in Hawaii. It is the largest volcano in the world.

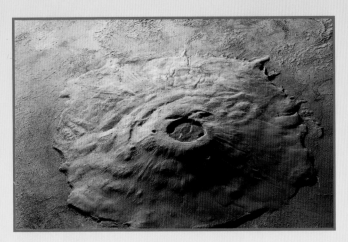

The planet Mars has a volcano called Mount Olympus. It is larger than volcanoes on Earth.

Picture glossary

cone the shape of the top of some volcanoes

crater the hole at the top of a volcano

lava hot liquid rock which erupts out of a volcano

Index

Notes to parents and teachers

Before reading
Talk about volcanoes. Explain that they are landforms which are made when hot liquid rock erupts through the Earth's crust. Have they ever seen a photo of a volcano or a film showing a volcano erupting?

After reading
Show the children how to draw a simple outline of a volcano with a crater on textured wallpaper. Tell them to add the red hot lava erupting out of the volcano using strips of red raffia or thin ribbon. Help the children to label the crater and the lava on the volcano. Make an erupting volcano! (NB. This is a messy activity which is best completed outside). What you need: one foil plate, 4 tablespoons of bicarbonate of soda, half a cup of vinegar, a few drops of washing up liquid, a small plastic bottle (no top), plasticine, a small funnel, red food colouring, half a cup of water, half a teaspoon of glitter (optional). What to do: Stand the bottle on the foil plate and shape the plasticine around the bottle to look like a volcano. Be careful not to let any plasticine get inside the bottle. Use the funnel to pour the bicarbonate of soda into the bottle. Add the washing up liquid and the water with the glitter. Add the red food colouring to the vinegar. Use the funnel to pour the vinegar mixture into the bottle. Quickly remove the funnel. Stand back and watch your volcano erupt!